SIMPLE SE

SIMPLE PRAYER

PRAY LIKE JESUS

STEPHEN J. ROBINSON

Simple Prayer: Pray Like Jesus

Copyright © 2021 by Stephen J. Robinson. All rights reserved.

Created and published under license to Church of the King, Incorporated d.b.a. COTK Publishing. Printed and manufactured in the United States of America.

Church of the King® is a registered service mark owned by Church of the King, Incorporated. COTK Publishing℠ is a service mark owned by Church of the King, Incorporated. Any use of any of the service marks of Church of the King, Incorporated without the prior written approval of Church of the King, Incorporated is prohibited.

Any copying, duplication, reproduction, republication, transmission, broadcasting, public display, distribution, dissemination, or storage in any retrieval system of this book, in whole or in part, by any means, method, or medium, is strictly prohibited apart from the prior, written consent of COTK Publishing.

Scripture taken from the New King James Version®. Copyright © 1982 by Thomas Nelson. Used by permission. All rights reserved.

ISBN 978-1-64219-014-4. Print edition.
ISBN 978-1-64219-015-1. E-book edition.

Submit reprint and other licensing requests to COTK Publishing, P.O. Box 2306, Mandeville, Louisiana, 70470, or to licensing@churchoftheking.com.

CONTENTS

CHAPTER 1:

YOU CAN ENJOY A POWERFUL PRAYER LIFE

"Once you have tasted the rewards of spending time alone with God, you won't be able to stay away."

— STEVE ROBINSON

In 1987, I put my faith in Jesus, and everything changed.

Those early years as a Christian were filled with purpose, inspiration, prayer, and deep healing in my soul. There was something very special going on in the church where I first came to Christ that became an integral part of my newfound freedom—and it's impacted my life every day since.

Early each morning, the church was filled with people praying. They beat the sunrise to meet with God before doing anything else. It was contagious! These dedicated people modeled prayer for me, showing the unlimited spiritual power that prayer can unleash in our lives. Just as important, my church's associate pastor and my small group leader mentored me in how to pray in those early years!

My prayer life started with the four simple verses in Matthew 6 that changed the course of history. Jesus shared what we know today as the *Lord's Prayer.* While it *seems* familiar to many of us, it proved revolutionary at the time (and still does today!). Jesus referring to God as His own Father majorly ruffled some religious leaders' feathers!

You see, Jesus didn't pray like anyone else in history. He explained in Matthew 6:5–7 that prayer isn't about using fancy phrases that make you sound spiritual. God doesn't care about profound words. Jesus also said prayer is more than just repeating lines that haven't sunk deep into our hearts. He told us we must mean what we say. The wonderful news is that He showed the disciples how to pray this way, and even today, we can follow along with them.

AT ITS HEART, PRAYER IS SIMPLE.

Maybe you feel stuck in your prayer life. Perhaps you've struggled to find the words. Or it might be that developing a daily prayer time has been years in the making but you just haven't cracked it. It's okay. I was there once—yet I learned how to pray. At its heart, prayer is simple. You can do it and you can start today.

We're going to spend the rest of this book helping you find power, clarity, and joy in daily prayer as His disciples. Now before charging ahead, let's read Jesus's revolutionary prayer!

Jesus said in Matthew 6:9–13:

> *In this manner, therefore, pray:*
>
> *Our Father in heaven, hallowed be Your name. Your kingdom come. Your will be done on earth as it is in heaven. Give us this day our daily bread. And forgive us our debts, as we forgive our debtors. And do not*

> *lead us into temptation, but deliver us from the evil one. For Yours is the kingdom and the power and the glory forever. Amen.*

Whether Jesus, Himself, prayed exactly like this every day, one thing we do know for sure from Scripture: He had an intimate daily prayer life with His Father. No doubt His disciples were in awe, seeing Him regularly connect with His Father, returning with overwhelming power, clarity, and joy. Jesus's personal relationship with His Father was thought to be impossible by those around Him. Now, let's push pause for just a moment. Can you relate to those people? Have you ever witnessed someone who seemed to have God's private cell number? It's easy to feel like a rich prayer life is reserved only for a few special people, *but not for us*. In fact, I remember having those same feelings after first becoming a Christian.

Prayer intimidated me. However, I quickly learned what Jesus was teaching the disciples: an extraordinary prayer life is possible for everyone who believes in Him. This is true for the youngest child to those of us who might have a little silver sneaking into our hairlines. How can I be sure of this, you ask?

In Luke 11:1, one of the disciples finally mustered up the courage to say to Jesus, "Lord, teach us to pray." Isn't that powerful? The disciples didn't know how to pray. They began at the same place I did in 1987. Their hearts longed to pray like Jesus—and He wanted that for them too. His instruction did not disappoint.

Jesus simplified prayer and made it accessible for His disciples. He does the same for us today. Prayer does not need to be complicated. Prayer is *talking* to God, prayer is *listening* to God, and prayer can follow a *simple pattern*.

THE DISCIPLES' PRAYER

With few exceptions, I've followed Jesus's prayer pattern every morning for the last thirty-two years! That's 11,680 meetings with God. This prayer pattern isn't like grade school clothes that fade at the knees and elbows. It doesn't get old or wear out. It gets better every day. In fact, it's taught me the simplest things are often some of the most profound. It's also clarified for me what prayer *is*—and what it *isn't*.

This reminds me of a fifth-grade boy who had listened to a sermon on persistence in prayer. One night, the boy was praying all alone in his room. As his dad passed his son's door, he heard the boy saying over and over again, "Tokyo. Tokyo. Tokyo." Curious, he entered his son's room and asked what he was doing. The boy replied that he had given the wrong answer on a test for the capital of Mexico, and he was praying *persistently* that God would make Tokyo its capital! This young man certainly had the persistence part down, but I think he was a little unclear on what prayer really is.

Prayer is more than asking God to fix things for us. Prayer is talking to God, listening to Him, and experiencing His presence and power in every area of your life. From praising Him to asking for provision, He loves hearing from us and answering our requests. Like Jesus said in John 14:13, "And whatever you ask in My name, that I will do, that the Father may be glorified in the Son."

God is a good Father who cares about you. He cares about the moms in Milwaukee and in Mumbai and the children in Alabama and in Afghanistan. The truth about prayer is that God is both able and willing. He can speak to all of us simultaneously. There are no limits to what God can do.

This also means prayer isn't a waste of time. Instead, it is the best use imaginable of our time. This is a tough pill to swallow for some, especially Type A personalities; people who fire off work

“

THERE ARE
NO LIMITS
TO WHAT GOD
CAN DO.

emails at 11:30 at night and are up at 5:30 the next morning, ready to charge straight back into the fray. People of this mindset feel like they have so much to do they can't make time to pray.

Now, let me be honest. I understand this well. *I am that Type A individual.* But some wisdom from an especially busy believer sticks with me. Around 500 years ago, the great church reformer Martin Luther started working early and kept on late into the night, but still made time for morning prayer for he had so much to do.

I HAVE SO MUCH TO DO TODAY THAT I SHALL SPEND THE FIRST THREE HOURS IN PRAYER.
– *MARTIN LUTHER*

I'm not saying you have to start with praying three hours, but I am saying there is a need for us to connect with God in prayer. Why not start with thirty minutes … or even three minutes?

What I've found is when we pray and connect with God first, we see our work in a different light. Why? Because we are walking in God's presence and in His power rather than operating on our own strength. Prayer increases your wisdom, discernment, and spiritual sensitivity. The best example of this in history is Jesus Himself.

DO YOU NEED GOD TO SPEAK TO YOU?

Maybe you're dealing with a challenging situation in your marriage right now. You need God to speak to you. Perhaps you are in a difficult situation with a loved one in your family. You need God to speak to you. Maybe you're making an important financial or business decision. You need God to speak to you.

God wants to speak to you! He wants you to pray, and then He wants you to hear what He has to say. This is why our prayer life is so important. Having a prayer life means we check in with headquarters, hear from Heaven, and get wisdom from God. Do you realize the advantages you have through prayer? Think about it! As Christians, we can hear from the God who knows everything.

I'm grateful that, when I was a young believer, prayer was both modeled for me and I was mentored in how to pray. I watched my pastors and fellow church members pray and then learned from my small group leader how to do it. In fact, this is exactly what Jesus did for the disciples; He was both model *and* mentor.

Every day I wake up in the morning ready to spend time with God in prayer. I've been doing this since I was nineteen. It's not about how long I spend in prayer but about taking the time to connect with God. Simply start somewhere.

Most of our lives are filled to the brim. You may have a demanding job that constantly floods outside of "working hours." You might be busy studying for exams. Perhaps you have a new baby who isn't very interested in sleep. Or it may seem like it's all you can do to get the kids to school and still make it to work on time!

Do you have a daily time when you connect with God? It doesn't have to be an hour, but could you start with any amount of time? There's something about a time of prayer each day, even five or ten minutes, that makes a difference in our lives. As a new believer, I was reading the Bible and came across something that blew me away. In Mark 1:35 we see this: "Now in the morning, having risen a long while before daylight, He [Jesus] went out and departed to a solitary place; and there He prayed."

I want you to *really* think about this for a moment.

Even though Jesus was 100 percent God, He was also 100 percent man. He took time early in the morning to connect with the Father and listen to Him. This is how He navigated life, and you would be hard-pressed to find anyone more productive than Jesus.

After all, He ministered to the multitudes, healed the sick, raised the dead, died on the cross, and was raised from the dead to pay the ultimate price for the sin of the world—all in just three years!

If Jesus needed to pray, how much more do we?

THREE STEPS TO A POWERFUL PRAYER LIFE

Day after day, Jesus's disciples watched Him connect with God. After He came back from spending time with the Father, there was fresh power and clarity in His life. He knew exactly what to do and how to do it.

Prayer helped Jesus:

- Know who to surround Himself with (Luke 6:12–16).
- Understand when it was time to move on (Mark 1:35–39).
- Feel His Father's compassion for people (Luke 19:41).
- Submit His plans to God (Luke 22:42).
- Experience the Father's pleasure in Him as His Son (Matthew 3:17).

These examples are just the tip of the iceberg. Would you like to enjoy the fresh power that comes from connecting with God in prayer? I know I would. Here's a simple way to explain how prayer can help us achieve this. Prayer connects us to God, who has all power. Prayer is not the power; it's the PVC pipe that connects us to the power. When we connect with God through prayer, power comes flowing into and through our lives!

PRAYER CONNECTS US TO GOD, WHO HAS ALL POWER.

In my experience, there are three steps to connecting with God's power every day. These are inspired by the first book I ever read about prayer called *Could You Not Tarry*

One Hour? Learning the Joy of Prayer by Larry Lea. I still revisit my tattered copy often. Through Lea's book, I learned three things you need to pray like Jesus: passion, practice, and pleasure.

PASSION FOR PRAYER

The first step to powerful prayer is passion.

Do you find it to be true in your life that most of the things you're really into are fueled by your passion? Most endeavors and adventures begin with passion. In our fast-paced lives, if we don't really want something, it's probably not going to happen. For example, we can desire to look and feel healthy, but is our passion for better health strong enough to pass on the tortilla chips at our favorite Mexican restaurant? That's when our passion is put to the test. Is your motivation to get healthier strong enough to get you out of bed and into the gym early in the morning?

In the same way, to have a thriving prayer life, you and I must *want* to pray. Desire and passion are the key. Jesus put it like this in Matthew 5:6: "Blessed are those who hunger and thirst for righteousness, for they shall be filled." My prayer for you is that a great passion and desire to pray will spark like a fire in your heart, burning so intense you will do whatever it takes to become a person of prayer. Whatever changes you need to make to your schedule to connect with God, it's time to make them.

PRACTICE IN PRAYER

The second step to building a life of prayer is practice.

We learn to pray by praying. The more time we spend praying to God, the more we grow in our prayer life. For example, you may play a musical instrument. To play that instrument well, you must practice … every day! That's why bands, orchestras, and musicians practice regularly. Similarly, succeeding in life, reaching all that God has for us, requires forming the habit of

“

TODAY IS A GREAT DAY TO BEGIN A DEEPER PRAYER LIFE.

consistently showing up before God to pray. To develop a prayer habit, start by choosing a time when you are alert and awake. At first, you might start with only five minutes of prayer, and then you can progress from there. Eventually, you will learn to pray for twenty minutes, thirty minutes, forty-five minutes, and then for an entire hour. Sound crazy?

My friend, I promise you, when you have a thriving prayer life, time melts away in God's presence. This isn't about legalism or following a rigid, religious structure in order to be accepted by God. It's about taking full advantage of our access to Him.

If up to this point in your life you've only prayed before a test, an important meeting, a meal, or in moments of crisis, that's okay. Today is a great day to begin a deeper prayer life. I invite you to set up an intentional prayer time. In fact, why don't you go ahead and write it down now?

My intentional prayer time with God will be at ___________ every day.

PLEASURE IN PRAYER

The third step to powerful prayer is experiencing the special pleasure found only in God's presence.

Once you have tasted the rewards of spending time alone with God, you won't be able to stay away. Time with God brings life to your soul. It's a daily time of refreshment, renewal, and richness in your spirit. Psalm 34:8 says, "Oh, taste and see that the LORD is good; Blessed is the man who trusts in Him!"

That's my goal for you in this book—allow God to teach you to pray. Allow me, as your guide, to help you on this journey. Begin to connect with Him, have a great passion for time with Him, and learn to take great pleasure in His presence.

Perhaps you can relate to the little boy at the beginning of the chapter asking God to change an answer on his test. In your life, maybe prayer has been reserved for emergencies and desperate requests. That can change today. If you'd like to become a person who prays daily—and enjoys it—*you can.*

Here's how we'll start down the path together. In the chapters ahead, we'll study the *Lord's Prayer* line by line, with these key phrases as our guides:

1. Our Father: Getting to Know God
2. Thy Kingdom Come: Seeking God's Will Over My Own
3. Daily Bread: Trusting God's Provision
4. Forgive: Releasing Toxic Anger, Unforgiveness, and Bitterness
5. Temptation: Overcoming Sin's Power Every Day
6. The Glory: Experiencing Gratitude for God's Goodness

Now, let's learn the first secret to praying like Jesus: *a relationship with the Father.*

REFLECTION QUESTIONS

Before you move on to the next chapter, take some time to reflect on these questions:

- *Why do you want to be a person of prayer?*
- *How will you make prayer a regular part of your day?*
- *In what ways do you believe God answers the prayers of His people?*
- *What answered prayers have you seen in your own life?*
- *What experiences have you had with the Lord's Prayer?*

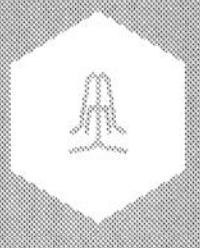

CHAPTER 2: OUR FATHER

"Prayer is the pathway that brings you closer to God."
— STEVE ROBINSON

When you hear the word *father*, what comes to mind?

For me, it triggers mixed emotions. I had a broken relationship with my biological father. He was an alcoholic, which made life difficult for our family. Our relationship was rocky at best—and outright hostile at worst.

At nineteen, when I encountered the *Lord's Prayer*, I realized my image of a father needed some repairs. It was like a once-beautiful building that had fire damage on the inside and hurricane damage on the outside. My father-image needed restoration. This became glaringly evident to me when Jesus jumped right into the deep end of the relational pool by addressing God as "Our Father."

In the thirty-plus years since meeting Jesus as my Savior, I've come to know God as the only perfect Father I'll ever meet.

However, it took some time. It took learning to understand exactly who God is. As I got to know Him better, I came to trust Him more.

In this chapter, I invite you on that same journey. Maybe you're like me and had a troubled relationship with your earthly father. Perhaps you're like the woman who once told me she avoided Father's Day weekend services because her father abused her. Or, maybe you're one of those blessed people who has enjoyed a good relationship with your earthly father.

Regardless of your past, praying like Jesus begins the process of renovating our old, hurtful concept of a father into who the good Father really is. It flips the script, unblocking our view of God from negative experiences with our earthly dads. As a father myself, I can tell you, there's no *perfect* parent but our Heavenly Father.

Let's meet our Father in Heaven afresh and get to know Him on a personal level in prayer. Let me tell you, friend, this relationship will anchor your soul, provide security, and flood your life with power. Our God is exactly who we need in every moment.

First, let's ask a question. Why did Jesus start with praying to a Father?

LOOK UP, NOT IN!

The disciples watched Jesus pray every day—and sometimes all night. But He didn't pray like anyone else. He didn't ramble, toss empty religious phrases into the sky, or get stuck. In fact, He would slip away for *hours*, praying early in the morning or evening. However, when Jesus returned from these prayer sessions, He walked in fresh power and purpose. When the disciples saw this, they effectively said, "We want that!"

When Jesus taught the disciples to pray, He ruffled some serious feathers. The religious folks of His day saw God as unapproachable; certainly not a dad! It was scandalous for Jesus to pray to God as Father—so scandalous that those offended spiritual leaders plotted to kill Him. They said by addressing God as Father, He made God His equal (John 5:18).

To add even more context, the Jewish people hadn't heard from God in centuries. The last book of the Old Testament, Malachi, had been written some 400 years before. The silent years were coming to an end.

It was time for the people to get fresh water from the wellspring of God's power and presence. Off the starting line, Jesus showed the disciples two powerful truths:

1. We are in a close, parent-child relationship with God as our good Father.
2. Every answer is found by looking up, not looking within.

First, we have the same Father as Jesus—and through His blood, we have 24/7 access to His attention *and* affection (Hebrews 4:16). Isn't that amazing? God isn't a distant Being in the sky, disinterested in our daily lives. He's a Father who always picks up the spiritual cell phone when we call!

JESUS SHOWED US THAT PRAYER ISN'T ABOUT GAZING *WITHIN*; IT'S ABOUT LOOKING UP!

Second, we don't discover life's deepest meaning or find ultimate help by looking in the mirror. Jesus showed us that prayer isn't about gazing *within*; it's about looking up! The answers to our most urgent questions and pressing problems aren't found inside of us. We don't light incense, sit on the floor, cross our legs, and empty our minds—we fall to our knees, look up, and open our spiritual ears.

Jesus gives a focal point: *pray to the Father.*

What is this Father like? Is He like the many earthly fathers who failed us? Is He an angry dad in the sky, waiting to zap us for every mistake? Is He too busy saving the world to listen to our "itty-bitty" problems? Or is He just a really nice person, unable to do more than listen?

Let me show you exactly what He's like. Here's what Scripture says in Colossians 1:15: Jesus "is the image of the invisible God, the firstborn over all creation." This means Jesus is the clearest picture of who God is. If we want to know the Father, we start by meeting His Son. Jesus was constantly helping, healing, and delivering people. He didn't put sickness and pain *on* people; He took sickness and pain *off* of people. He didn't pile guilt *on* people, He took guilt *off* of people. He didn't take *from* people; He gave *to* people.

Why? Because God is a good Father! He isn't a disconnected killjoy. He's not scheming to take anything from us. Instead, He comes as a servant, giving everything, knowing full well we can't give Him anything of equal value in return. This is a Father who loves us at great expense—*even giving His own Son.*

Believe it or not, it gets even better. Because not only did Jesus die on the cross in our place, but three days later, the Father raised Him from the dead (Acts 10:40). I don't know where you come from, but here in New Orleans, that's not normal! As a rule, dead people stay dead.

So not only is our Father good, but He is powerful. If He's powerful enough to bring the dead back to life, imagine what He can do for you.

Our starting point in developing a powerful prayer life begins with a fresh perspective of God.

How we view God determines how we pursue Him. Your perspective is like your car's windshield. If your windshield gets splattered with mud and bugs, it gets a little tough to see. Perhaps you've heard and experienced some things in life that have flung

“

HOW WE VIEW GOD DETERMINES HOW WE PURSUE HIM.

mud onto your perspective of God. It's time to switch on the wipers and get a clear picture of God.

We get this by looking at Jesus and seeing His character. As we do, there's an invitation to go even deeper.

HELLO, MY NAME IS ...

If we met for the first time, we would probably ask each other, "What's your name?" Names provide unique identities, distinguishing us from others.

Did you know God introduces Himself by many different names in Scripture? As a young Christian, this surprised me. I wondered if God had some sort of identity crisis! But I learned that just like sparkling facets on a diamond, God's names reveal different facets of His nature.

His names express who He is *and* what He does.

Way back in Genesis 22, we read a peculiar story about a man named Abraham and his teenage son, Isaac. They went on a hike together—but it was no ordinary walk up a mountain. God aked Abraham to sacrifice Isaac when they reached the summit to test his faith. That's scary stuff! But Abraham packed up, trusting in God that this crazy request would make sense.

After three days, they reached the base of the mountain. Abraham split wood and Isaac carried it—the very wood he was to be sacrificed on. The father and son got to the mountaintop, built the altar, and Abraham raised a knife to do the unthinkable! But just before he struck, the Angel of the Lord called out to Abraham, telling him to stop. At that very instant, he saw a ram in the thicket that became the sacrifice instead of Isaac. God never intended for Abraham to go through with it.

That day was so important because Abraham called God by the name Jehovah-Jireh, or "the LORD will provide." God was exactly what Abraham and Isaac needed in that moment.

What makes all this so fascinating is the fact that Isaac was a precursor of Jesus carrying the cross (the wood) He would be sacrificed on a hill—that very same hill—later called Golgotha.

God, our Good Father, gave us His *only* Son to die in our place. We need a provider—and that is who He is!

God's names are found throughout the Old Testament. To a great leader named Moses, He said in Exodus 15:26, "*I am* the LORD who heals you." In Hebrew, that name is Jehovah-Rapha. To the famous King David, God revealed Himself as Shepherd, Jehovah-Rohi.

God's names are tied to His character and actions.

GOD'S NAMES ARE TIED TO HIS CHARACTER AND ACTIONS.

Today, God still says to us, His children, that He is to us what we need Him to be! If you're sick, He's your healer. If you are lost, He's your Shepherd—guiding you home. If you are tormented, He can be your banner of deliverance. If you are drowning in sin, He is your righteousness.

Prayer is our means of meeting with the God who meets our needs.

EMBRACE THE PROMISES OF GOD

Jesus called God by a new name in Matthew 6:9, giving a fresh revelation of who He is: *our Father.* Jesus shows a new dynamic in God's relationship with His people. And because Jesus is our mentor and model, we should start in the same place He did, praying to our good Father.

Let me invite you into a practice that will electrify your prayer life—praying through the names of God. Why? His names validate His promises. Just as God as Father reveals our position with Him and His heart for us as children, Scripture shares other names that showcase God's character.

They might sound a little funny or hard to pronounce. But don't worry, no one's listening but God, and He won't mind. I've prayed through these eight names countless times and in just about every place imaginable—even in my driveway. No matter where you are, these names are powerful because they help us look *up* and not just *in*.

Following Jesus's model, here's how I've incorporated this into my prayer life. I say the name of God, what it means, and declare that action in my life. Just as God provided for Abraham, I believe His provision for me. As He healed Moses, I believe His healing is for me. As He was David's Shepherd, I believe He's leading us still today. Let's pray through these together so you can start this practice for yourself.

1. **Jehovah-Tsidkenu:** *The LORD, my righteousness.*
   "God, You make me clean! You wipe away my sin, guilt, and shame. You are perfect, and You have made a way for an imperfect person like me to be Your child. Thank you for the blood of Jesus that does for me what I could never do for myself."
2. **Jehovah-Mekaddishkem:** *The Lord, my sanctification.*
   "God, You make me holy. You've set me apart for your work today. You clean me up and are making me more like Jesus. I repent of my bad attitudes, sinful choices, and wrong actions. Thank You for making me into a new person every day!"
3. **Jehovah-Shammah:** *The Lord is near.*
   "God, You are with me. I don't walk through this day on my own. You don't live far away in a temple; You live in me! Even though I feel alone today, I know You are near. Thank You for being my constant companion."

4. **Jehovah-Shalom:** *The Lord, my peace.*
   "God, when I feel anxious today, thank You for bringing me comfort. Thank You for Your peace that surpasses all knowledge and understanding. My stress can melt away because You have everything under control. Jesus, You are the Prince of Peace, and I invite Your peace into every relationship and area of my life. I believe You are the only One who can calm every storm."
5. **Jehovah-Rapha:** *The Lord, my healer.*
   "God, You have power to raise the dead and power to heal my body, mind, emotions, and relationships. You are a Good Father who wants us to be whole. Thank You for healing us. I believe You are working miracles of healing today."
6. **Jehovah-Jireh:** *The Lord, my provision.*
   "God, meet me in my work and provide for me. I believe You will give me everything I need, even when I don't see how."
7. **Jehovah-Nissi:** *The Lord, my banner.*
   "God, thank You for victory! Thank You for fighting my battles and winning. I won't be afraid, because no matter what comes against me today, You are the only Warrior who never loses. You are on my side!"
8. **Jehovah-Roi:** *The Lord, my shepherd.*
   "God, like a watchful shepherd, You watch over me. You keep me from falling off the cliffs of life. You lead me to calm waters. You care for me. You guide me, steady and sure. I know You are always a step ahead and will give me clarity on exactly what to do next. I will follow Your voice today."

I encourage you to pray through God's names every day. This will take you deeper into the heart of our Good Father. He never separates who He is from what He does. I promise this is a faith and relationship builder like you've never experienced.

These times in prayer will be like your spiritual windshield wipers, reminding you exactly who God is. It removes the mud and grime blocking our view. No matter what your earthly father was like, you have a loving, perfect, and powerful Father in Heaven.

As you meet Him, your good, good Father, you will experience those names becoming a loving reality in your life. You will see Heaven unleashed in your life. And that brings us to the next phrase in the prayer pattern Jesus teaches us. Get ready to bring the power of Heaven to Earth.

REFLECTION QUESTIONS

Before moving on to the next chapter, take some time to reflect on these questions.

- *When you think of God the Father, what comes to mind?*
- *How would you describe Him as a Father?*
- *What did you learn about God while reading this chapter?*
- *Think about the eight names of God we prayed through. Which one resonates with you most? Why?*
- *Which name of God will be the easiest to pray? Why?*
- *Which name of God will be the most difficult to pray? Why?*

CHAPTER 3:

YOUR KINGDOM COME

"When we pray, 'Your kingdom come,' we are asking Jesus to establish His rulership in our lives, families, and world."

— STEVE ROBINSON

Jesus had a habit of sneaking away to be alone. He did this early in the morning, late in the evening, and even after exhausting interactions—like feeding five thousand people. The disciples watched His pattern carefully, and it always looked the same. Jesus withdrew, then returned with renewed power.

I'm sure they wondered what on Earth He was praying about. He always came back from prayer with fresh anointing, authority, and direction on *exactly* what they needed to do next.

In Luke 11:1, we read of one of the disciples finally working up the nerve to ask Jesus to teach them His secret to prayer. That's when Jesus taught them the pattern we're studying together now.

We just learned to pray to God as our good Father. Now we move to the next topic, and it is where Jesus's amazing anointing and power came from: the Kingdom of God. My friend, if you'd like a new dimension of God's power unleashed in your life, welcome to the source. As Jesus prayed, He *asked* for Heaven to invade Earth. He invited God's Kingdom to be the directing force in His life, His followers' lives, and the entire world. While there is mystery to this kingdom, there are tangible realities we can grab a hold of. We can partner with God, aligning ourselves with His desires, making them our own.

What exactly is the Kingdom of God we're supposed to invite?

WHAT IS THE KINGDOM OF GOD?

Here's a simple definition: *The Kingdom of God is the rule and reign of God.* The Kingdom, or the rule of God, is present in the hearts of His people. God's Kingdom has a King. That King is Jesus, and everything in the Kingdom is under His rule and influence.

Now, for those who live in the United States like I do, the idea of a kingdom can seem a little strange. After all, we live in a republic. We elect officials who represent our interests and vote them into or out of office. A true kingdom, though, is run by a king or queen who is the sole authority in the land. He or she has the final say on everything. What the king or queen says, goes!

The Kingdom of God operates like this. Only instead of a physical kingdom, like the Jewish people expected (Acts 1:6), it's a spiritual kingdom. When Jesus said, "The kingdom of God is at hand" in Mark 1:15, He wasn't saying a golden throne was about to drop from the sky. Instead, He meant that God's rule and reign was available in our hearts. The supernatural was invading the natural.

Let me tell you friends, having a King like Jesus, Who is perfectly good and gave everything for our salvation, is the greatest news we can receive. The secret to spiritual power is not just prayer—it's prayer that *connects us* to God and His Kingdom, purpose, and power.

In this chapter, we're going to ask God to flood His Kingdom into four key areas: ourselves, our families, our church, and our nation. Do you think these could be better with a little more Heaven in them? I sure do. Let's begin with the most important place for Heaven to have its way: in our own lives.

PRAYING FOR THE KINGDOM OF GOD TO BE ESTABLISHED IN OUR LIVES

Every plane flight starts the same. Once the cabin door closes, the flight attendants walk the passengers through the safety procedures in case of an emergency. They explain how to buckle and unbuckle your seatbelt. They point to exit rows and tell you what to do in case the plane loses pressure. Oxygen masks will drop down from the ceiling so everyone can breathe.

What do they say? "*Put your own oxygen mask on first before trying to help anyone else.*"

You have to make sure your body gets enough oxygen to avoid passing out. After all, you won't be much help to others if you're unconscious!

I've found our spiritual lives are the same way. Hard times come. People hurt us. And sometimes, it feels like all of the air goes whooshing out our lives. Guess what we need to do? Put our own spiritual oxygen masks on first.

That's why, every morning, I pray God's Kingdom into my own life first before praying over anyone else. This is how we should all pray—not to be selfish, but so we have the spiritual power necessary to do Kingdom work in this world. Our own lives need to be aligned with Heaven's agenda instead of our own! The world is filled with distractions and disappointments, so it is essential we check in with headquarters for daily direction.

Jesus prayed this way, "Your kingdom come. Your will be done on earth as *it is* in heaven" (Luke 11:1b). Here's how this sounds for me, "God, let your kingdom come, and your will be done … *in my life today*."

I'm breathing in God's spiritual oxygen. As I pray, I'm declaring I want God's will to rule in every nook-and-cranny of my life.

You see, as followers of Christ, being born again is not only about eternal salvation, it's also about allowing God's rule in our lives. It's about submitting our wants to God's will. When we pray "Your kingdom come," we place God on the throne of our hearts to rule our spirits, souls, and bodies.

OUR OWN LIVES NEED TO BE ALIGNED WITH HEAVEN'S AGENDA INSTEAD OF OUR OWN!

We also see Jesus model this in prayer and submission to the Father's will in the Garden of Gethsemane. In Luke 22:42, He prayed, "Father, if it is Your will, take this cup away from Me; nevertheless, not My will, but Yours, be done." As a man, Jesus did not want to go to the cross. He knew torment, agony, and sorrow waited for Him on that hill. However, He honored the Father's will over His wants—this is the epitome of Kingdom living.

The result? Jesus redeemed us and was glorified, being seated at the right hand of God (Colossians 3:1).

Through prayer, God will show you any areas of self-will, rebellion, or stubbornness. Confess these to Him. Allow Him to remove anything from your life that keeps you from wholeheartedly serving Him.

“

HERE’S THE PROMISE: WHEN WE PRAY IN ALIGNMENT WITH GOD’S WILL, IT CAN’T HELP BUT HAPPEN!

PRAYING FOR THE KINGDOM OF GOD TO BE ESTABLISHED IN OUR FAMILIES

After putting on our spiritual oxygen masks, our next priority for God's rule is in our family, praying, "Your kingdom come, your will be done … *in my family*." We ask for God's righteousness, peace, and joy to fill their lives.

Every morning, I pray for my wife and four children by name. I ask God to give me insight and wisdom for each of their lives. If you are married, pray for your spouse. If you have children or grandchildren, pray that God's Kingdom will be established in their lives. Pray over your family's spouses if they are married. If they're not married, don't forget to pray for their future spouse.

As I write this, I have children from grade school to graduate school! I pray over them; I make specific requests and declarations over their lives. Oftentimes, I quote Job 22:28, "You will also declare a thing, and it will be established for you; so light will shine on your ways."

Here's the promise: When we pray in alignment with God's will, it can't help but happen!

When we're faithful in praying for our family, amazing things happen. Not only does God intervene to guide and provide for them, but broken relationships begin to be repaired. The fastest way to change your heart toward a family member, or their heart toward you, is to pray for them.

PRAYING FOR THE KINGDOM OF GOD TO BE ESTABLISHED IN OUR CHURCH

No matter how many biological or adopted family members you have, you're part of an even larger family *billions* strong: the family of God. The Apostle Paul wrote in Ephesians 2:19, "Now, therefore, you are no longer strangers and foreigners, but fellow citizens with the saints and members of the household of God."

So, we pray, "Your kingdom come, your will be done … *in my church family*."

Our mission as a church family is reaching people and building lives. We certainly want to impact the world—but we first focus on the areas where God has planted us. There is a reason each one of us lives where we do. In God's providence, you are where you are. For this reason, we invite people from our city and region into God's Kingdom through the blood of Jesus Christ.

Do you know how we do that? Every one of us needs to be submitted to and guided by the Holy Spirit. We need to look at our communities through God's eyes. We need a fresh outpouring of God's power, and let me tell you, this requires that we pray for one another!

Pray for the pastors, the leadership team, the faithfulness of the people, and the harvest.

Here are a few of the ways you can specifically pray for your church:

Pray for your pastors. I'll admit, as a pastor myself, this may sound a little self-serving. But there is simply no way we can lead God's family without prayer over our own lives. As you pray for your pastor(s), ask God to empower them to lead well, deliver His word, and instill fresh vision.

Pray for the leadership team. By name, pray for your church leaders. A great starting point is with the people whose ministry work directly touches your life. As you pray for them, the Holy Spirit will often show you specific needs or give you a word of encouragement for them. Ask for health, unity, vision, and for God to have His way in every ministry of the church—starting with the leaders.

Pray for a faithful church. The church isn't a building; it's the people. When we pray for our church, we're praying for every person who gathers to worship with us. God's Kingdom rule creates faithful servants. We need God's power to live faithfully in every place: our homes, our workplaces, our community organizations, and everywhere else we find ourselves.

The hallmark of a faithful church is dedication to God's Kingdom, *especially* outside of our weekend services. God works through us 24/7, 365. As Paul wrote in 1 Corinthians 12:27, "Now you are the body of Christ, and members individually." As a church family, our purpose is to represent Jesus in our communities at all times.

Pray for the harvest. Jesus used interesting language about people coming to know Him as Savior and King. In Biblical times, people lived in an agrarian society, so Jesus used relevant analogies for them to understand His teaching. In Matthew 9:38, He said, "Therefore, pray to the Lord of the harvest to send out laborers into His harvest." We know the harvest comes at the end of the growing season. It's the whole point of planting seeds, watering the developing crops, and nurturing them.

The analogy here is that the Holy Spirit is working on people! He's working on your neighbors, co-workers, and the people who walk by you in the grocery store. It's planting and growing season—and soon, time for the harvest. When we pray for God's Kingdom in our communities, we're asking for the church family to reach out and welcome people into the family because the Holy Spirit's work is ripe!

With authority, pray that people will be saved, planted, established, strengthened, and rooted in the local church. Ask the Holy Spirit, the Lord of the harvest, to draw people to Jesus through the faithful work of the church.

PRAYING FOR THE KINGDOM OF GOD TO BE ESTABLISHED IN OUR NATION

Have you noticed an inward-out pattern? We begin by inviting God's Kingdom into our own lives, then our families, then our church and community; and finally, we ask for His will in our nation. Whether we voted for our current leaders or not, God commands us to pray for those in authority. First Timothy 2:1–2 says, "Therefore I exhort first of all that supplications, prayers, intercessions, and giving of thanks be made for all men, for kings and all who are in authority, that we may lead a quiet and peaceable life in all godliness and reverence."

Pray: "Your kingdom come, your will be done ... *in my nation*."

Pray the president will govern with wisdom, peace, and justice. Pray our leaders will walk in integrity, knowledge, and understanding. Ask that they learn to be people of prayer and faithful stewards of their authority. Intercede for them personally, as they navigate through sickness, family tragedies, fear, indecision, and everything else all of us experience at some point in our lives.

As you pray for the harvest locally, pray for spiritual renewal, revival, and awakening in your nation. Whether you live in the United States, like me, or anywhere else in the world, pray that people in your country turn to God.

God's heart is for every person to meet Jesus and experience salvation (2 Peter 3:9). This is why praying for God's rule and reign to sweep our world is powerful. Even though we may have different countries on our passports, God's family doesn't first belong to the geographical nations we live within; we are people of His Kingdom.

BRING IT TOGETHER IN PRAYER

Remember, the Kingdom of God is found wherever He rules and reigns in people's hearts. This Kingdom is more real than any kingdom or country that has ever existed. God's Kingdom is alive and eternal.

Just like Jesus, we ask for this everlasting Kingdom to be the governing force in our lives. Pray for His Kingdom to come in your life, your family, your church and community, and your nation.

GOD'S KINGDOM IS ALIVE AND ETERNAL.

As you do this day after day, you will see amazing things happen. We serve a good and powerful King whose heart is to heal and save. Let's ask for that reality to show up in every interaction we have. The great theologian George Ladd best summarized this thought: "What is the object of our quest? The Church? Heaven? No. We are to seek God's righteousness—His sway, His rule, His reign in our lives."[1]

REFLECTION QUESTIONS

Before moving on to the next chapter, take some time to reflect on these questions:

- *What do you think of when you hear the word kingdom?*
- *In your own life, how do you feel you have let the Kingdom of God reign?*
- *How is Jesus the King of your personal life?*

---

[1]George Eldon Ladd, *The Gospel of the Kingdom: Scriptural Studies in the Kingdom of God* (Eerdmans, 2011).

- *How can you pray for your church leadership and church family?*
- *In your nation, how might you pray for God to reign?*
- *What did you learn from this chapter about prayer and about the Kingdom of God?*

CHAPTER 4:

DAILY BREAD

"When we realize God is our sole Source, we will see Him add the super to our natural."

— STEVE ROBINSON

There's an old story about an aging widow who lived on a fixed income. She often found herself strapped financially. One day, as she was praying, she asked God to provide food. The poor widow had more month left than money. She cried out, "God, give me today my daily bread." Her landlord was constantly belittling her efforts in prayer. Walking by that morning, he heard her praying and thought to himself, *I'll show her once and for all that her prayers don't do any good.*

That afternoon, she left her apartment hungry, looking for any food scraps she could find. Meanwhile, her landlord went to the store and spent several hundred dollars stocking up her pantry. He folded his arms and leaned up against the wall in the hallway just outside of her apartment door, smirking.

When she returned to her apartment, she was blown away to find more than enough food! She loudly thanked God for His amazing provision. When he heard this, her landlord knocked on the door, excited to gloat. She answered the door, and immediately, her landlord said, "You're thanking God for all of your food—but He didn't provide it, I did! I bought everything with my own money, not God's."

He stood triumphantly, impressed with his cleverness.

The woman just smiled and said, "Well, the devil might have delivered it, but God sent it!" While that's a funny punchline, isn't it true? God provides everything we need, and often in surprising ways. Sometimes He uses unusual delivery methods, but He always takes care of His children.

In the *Lord's Prayer*, Jesus prayed in Luke 11:3, "Give us day by day our daily bread." He taught the disciples to ask for provision day by day. No matter if He provides through a hard day's work, a mischievous landlord, or miraculous means, as we learned in Chapter Two, our God is Jehovah-Jireh; He will provide. The question is, do you know how to ask for your daily provision?

DAILY BREAD, NIGHTLY QUAIL

Most of us have lived through seasons when money was tight. You may be in one of those right now. Have you ever been in a situation where you didn't know if your family could make ends meet or pay the bills? This is a nerve-wracking, stressful situation to be in. In Exodus 16, the Israelites found themselves in a circumstance where they didn't even know where their next meal would come from.

God miraculously freed them from slavery in Egypt. In a dramatic climax, they escaped the Egyptian army by crossing the Red Sea at night after God used Moses to part the water.

He saved them at the last moment. However, fast forward a few chapters in Exodus. We find God's people trudging along in the desert, saying in Exodus 16:3, "Oh, that we had died by the hand of the LORD in the land of Egypt, when we sat by the pots of meat and when we ate bread to the full! For you have brought us out into this wilderness to kill this whole assembly with hunger."

They were hungry! It turned out there weren't many buffets in the rugged wilderness. At the end of their ropes, many of them had all but given up.

Then God spoke with Moses. He heard their desperation and met His people with remarkable provision. Every evening, God provided quail. Every morning, He gave them bread. Do you know how much they had? Exactly what every person needed to live—for that day.

God's purpose in these daily gifts was even richer than filling their stomachs; He wanted to be in close relationship with them. God told Moses His daily provision was to "test them," to see if they would walk in the way He'd instructed them to live (Exodus 16:4). As a good Father, His laws were to keep them safe, holy before Him, and close as His children.

In Matthew 4:4, Jesus deepens our understanding of God's provision. While fasting in the wilderness, He was hungry. Satan came, tempting Him to break His fast by turning nearby stones into bread. But Jesus had an interesting response. Quoting Deuteronomy 8:3, He said, "It is written, 'Man shall not live by bread alone, but by every word that proceeds from the mouth of God.'" Jesus shows us there is a double meaning in God's provision. God promises both physical sustenance and spiritual nourishment. He cares for our physical needs—but more importantly, He provides daily spiritual nourishment through His Word. With God, the two always go together.

WALK CLOSELY WITH GOD

This is an encouraging history lesson, and it's a perfect picture of God's power to provide. God's physical provision helps us walk closely with Him. After all, a gift at just the right moment is a great springboard for grateful hearts that love the Giver Himself.

Being close to God implies a few things. It means understanding God's daily bread is provided as spiritual nourishment in His Word. It means fellowship with Jesus through a consistent and personal prayer life. It means daily sitting at our Master's feet, learning His ways. And when we walk closely with God, we'll also fellowship with each other. In the Garden of Eden, God created Eve so Adam wouldn't be alone—humans were created to be together.

Now, while Adam was created for community, he was also created to work (Genesis 2:15)! This is a primary means of God's provision. This positions us for God to bring His supernatural power to our natural effort. In fact, the thread of a healthy work ethic carries all the way through the Bible. Paul wrote to a church in a city called Thessalonica, "That you also aspire to lead a quiet life, to mind your own business, and to work with your own hands, as we commanded you, that you may walk properly toward those who are outside, and that you may lack nothing" (1 Thessalonians 4:11–12).

God gave us talents and abilities so we can work and be productive. Rather than self-reliance, work is a partnership with God.

Many times we have a wrong perspective of God's provision because we have a wrong perspective of work. When the children of Israel were in the wilderness, there was miraculous provision as the bread and quail appeared at their front doors. As soon as they stepped into the Promised Land, the meat and bread didn't show up on the dinner table any longer.

"

GOD GAVE US TALENTS AND ABILITIES SO WE CAN WORK AND BE PRODUCTIVE.

The people now had land and fields to plant crops and harvest their own food. Work is both a *good thing* and a *God thing* when balanced with His gift of Sabbath, or a day of rest. God supernaturally provides our daily bread to keep us close to Himself and allow us to be generous with one another.

THROUGH PRAYER, WE ALSO INVITE THE HOLY SPIRIT'S ACTIVITY INTO OUR WORK.

Through prayer, we also invite the Holy Spirit's activity into our work. This is a distinct advantage for Christians. We can ask God to bless our work, give us inspired ideas, and partner with us to make an eternal impact. Prayer floods God's power into our jobs like ocean waves that never stop coming. Pray for your co-workers, organization, and boss. God made us to work, and in prayer, He meets us there.

BE LASER-FOCUSED

During His ministry on Earth, Jesus was frequently followed by mobs of people—today they would all have their smartphones out, taking selfies, and posting them on social media. In Matthew 20:29–34, we read about one of those times. Crowds of thousands trailed Him, which I imagine would have been pretty noisy. However, Jesus heard two voices cut through the chatter, saying, "Have mercy on us, O Lord, Son of David!"

The swarming crowd hushed them, wanting to get on with their gawking. In the middle of all the movement and chaos, Jesus came to a dead stop, speaking directly to them. He looked them in the eyes and asked, "What do you want Me to do for you?"

Isn't that a stunning moment?

Out of the thousands pressing around Him, Jesus heard two men asking for mercy. Then He went a step further, asking them to get specific. It was time for them to be *laser-focused* on what they wanted.

Have you ever thought about praying laser-focused prayers, setting your spiritual sights on exactly what you want and need?

These two men were blind. When they heard Jesus passing by, they knew this was their chance to ask Him to cure their blindness. Verse 34 tells us, "So Jesus had compassion and touched their eyes. And immediately their eyes received sight, and they followed Him."

I *love* this! Check out the progression here:

- They had a need to receive their sight.
- They went to Jesus, the One they believed had the power to provide it.
- They were laser-focused, asking for exactly what they needed.
- They were healed, being drawn closer to Jesus by His provision.

When our church was young, we had a *serious* and *specific* need. Our church was a toddler, only eighteen months old at the time. We were growing, God was moving, and the momentum seemed unstoppable … until we were faced with a need to purchase a new property to make room for all the people coming to the church.

The problem was, we didn't have the money to make the down payment on the new property. We decided to list for sale another piece of property we owned to make the down payment on the new property.

To find the money, we prayed to *Jehovah-Jireh*—God, our Provider. We came together *in unity* to pray. Many of us gathered at noon for three days in a row to pray, laser-focused on getting the old property sold so we could buy the new one.

One day went by … no buyer.

Two days went by … still nothing.

On the third day, the clock was ticking. We didn't have any more time to come up with the funds, and the new property we believed God had called us to move on (it was like our own mini-Promised Land) was about to slip away.

At the last minute, God stepped in, doing what only He could do. Out of nowhere someone stepped up and wanted to purchase the property and close within days.

Do you know how much it sold for? Exactly the remaining balance we needed for the down payment!

We prayed laser-focused prayers. As if turning to look at us in the midst of a great crowd, God heard our cries, saw our specific need, and wrote the proverbial check!

What do you want or need right now? Get laser-focused in prayer for your daily bread.

DON'T GIVE UP

Now, let me draw your attention to one detail in that provision story: We met for three days in a row, and most of the time, nothing happened. We checked every morning, but no manna had fallen onto our lawns.

What if we had gotten discouraged and stopped asking on Day One, Day Two, or even at the beginning of Day Three?

You see, Jesus taught us in Matthew 7:7 not to give up in prayer, saying, "Ask, and it will be given to you; seek, and you will find; knock, and it will be opened to you."

The literal translation of this verse is not a one-and-done prayer. In the original language, it means to ask and keep on asking, seek and keep on seeking, and knock and keep on knocking. In prayer, we bang on heaven's door until it swings open.

God's children don't quit. When we're walking close to God and praying laser-focused prayers for what we need, we know He will provide. Jesus told the disciples in John 14:14, "If you ask anything in My name, *I will do it.*"

GOD'S CHILDREN DON'T QUIT.

Asking in Jesus's name means asking according to His character and will. Just like we did as a young church being laser-focused in prayer, I encourage you to pray specifically. The truth is, many give up right before the breakthrough. My friend, keep asking, seeking, and knocking. I believe your daily bread, God's provision in your life, is just on the other side of Heaven's door.

REFLECTION QUESTIONS

Before moving on to the next chapter, take some time to reflect on these questions:

- *Why do you believe God wants to provide for you in every way? Or, why don't you?*
- *Have you invited the Holy Spirit into your work life?*
- *How are you laser-focused in what you ask for?*
- *How have you given up or stayed persistent?*
- *What is one request you need to make to God today, tomorrow, and the next day?*
- *What did you learn from this chapter about prayer and God's provision for your daily bread?*

CHAPTER 5: FORGIVE US

"When you forgive, you unlock God's power in your life."

— STEVE ROBINSON

Certain verses in Scripture cause you to do a double-take the first time you read them. Some surprising, even incredible, things happen in every book of the Bible. However, there are two verses in Mark 11 that have always made me take a deep breath and pause a moment to process their gravity.

I'll set the scene.

Jesus was talking to His disciples after they noticed something curious. The day before, Jesus was hungry. He saw a nearby fig tree and walked over to pick some figs. When He arrived, ready to eat, He realized the tree had nothing but leaves—how disappointing! In Mark 11:14, we read Jesus's unhappy response: "'Let no one eat fruit from you ever again.' And His disciples heard it."

The next day, His disciples saw that very fig tree. Peter said in verse 21, "Rabbi, look! The fig tree which You cursed has withered away." Jesus used His power over nature as proof that they can have faith and "whatever things you ask when you pray, believe that you receive *them*, and you will have *them*" (Mark 11:24).

That's an interesting, faith-building story, right? Jesus has power over nature and promises God will answer faithful prayers. However, what He says next, in verses 24 and 25, is what stops me in my tracks: "And whenever you stand praying, if you have anything against anyone, forgive him, that your Father in heaven may also forgive you your trespasses. But if you do not forgive, neither will your Father in heaven forgive your trespasses."

If you're a little tired right now, grab a cup of coffee and read those verses again—*they are that important.* Jesus shows us two things:

1. If we don't forgive, we won't be forgiven.
2. God's power in our prayer lives is blocked when we hold on to unforgiveness.

Here's an image that has helped me apply these verses in my own life through the years.

Think of your life like a large PVC pipe. Imagine water flowing through unhindered. This represents God's power and presence in your life. Now, picture the flow stopping, without even the tiniest trickle. That's what happens when we harbor unforgiveness against someone else—it clogs the PVC pipe and robs us of God's power in our prayer lives.

The fastest way to block miracles in your life is to hold on to anger, bitterness, and grudges. This is serious business—and it was incredibly difficult for me personally to come to terms with this as a new Christian.

I carried a lot of hurt and bitterness in my heart toward my birth father. And the truth was, I felt justified in holding on to that bitterness. He said and did some cruel things to me, things I certainly would never say to my children. *How could a father treat his son like that?* I thought.

Little did I know, my spiritual PVC pipe was clogged, blocking God's power from flowing into my life.

DISCIPLES EXTEND GRACE

Over time, I learned that forgiven people forgive people. While hurt people *hurt people*, free people *free people.* God's people are grace extenders. In Jesus, we are forgiven of every evil thought, action, and inaction we've ever committed.

Scripture tells us that our scarlet sins are washed white as snow (Isaiah 1:18). Paul wrote that we are new creations in Christ, totally redeemed (2 Corinthians 5:17). Then, he took it a step further, saying in the very next verse, "Now all things *are* of God, who has reconciled us to Himself through Jesus Christ, and has given us the ministry of reconciliation."

HERE'S THE PATTERN: GOD FORGIVES US, THEN WE TURN AROUND AND EXTEND GRACE AND FORGIVENESS TO OTHERS.

In this context, reconciliation means restored relationships on two levels: between us and God, and between us and others. Here's the pattern: God forgives us, then we turn around and extend grace and forgiveness to others. As Christians, we shouldn't keep a death grip on anger, bitterness, or resentment against other people.

Now, you may be saying, "Pastor Steve, this sounds all well and good, but you don't understand how badly I've been wronged! How can I forgive people who've done such terrible things?"

Believe me when I tell you I *know* this is easier said than done. However, I believe you're reading this because you desire God's power to flood in and through your life. This means we need to unclog our spiritual PVC pipes. Let me share with you three practical ways to experience forgiveness so that your prayers will not be hindered.

ONE: ASK GOD TO FORGIVE YOU

As we pray to our Father about this topic of forgiveness, Jesus shows us we must ask God to "forgive us our sins." We don't start by pointing fingers at anyone else for their sin. We ask God to forgive us of our sins before we worry about anyone else.

First, this means putting your trust in Jesus as your Savior. Paul unpacks this process plainly in Romans 10:9: "that if you confess with your mouth the Lord Jesus and believe in your heart that God has raised Him from the dead, you will be saved." When we come to the Father in faith, realizing we can never deal with our sin on our own, and declare Jesus as our Savior, God welcomes us into His family.

Second, this means practicing a lifestyle of repentance. Anyone who has been a Christian for even a few days knows sin doesn't evaporate like rain on a sunny day. The word *repentance* simply means to turn around and go the other way. When we do sin, and then confess our sin, Jesus will forgive our sins. The Holy Spirit convicts us of our sin and guides us to a reset with God—repentance. We then experience forgiveness, and Christ gives us freedom from the sins weighing us down. Scripture teaches that we *can* lay aside "the sin which so easily ensnares us" (Hebrews 12:1).

Imagine a marathon runner jogging twenty-six miles with a heavy, weighted vest. Wouldn't that be crazy? In the same way, when we carry the weight of sin day after day, our spirits suffocate. Jesus invites us into forgiveness and freedom from that weighted vest. From personal experience, the Holy Spirit puts a finger on the sin we need to lay aside! This is a beautiful daily practice.

If unconfessed sin (which is sin we've either ignored or been ignorant of) surfaces at this point, confess that sin to God. Claim this promise from 1 John 1:9: "If we confess our sins, He is faithful and just to forgive us our sins and to cleanse us from all unrighteousness."

The word *confess* in 1 John 1:9 means "to speak the same thing." In other words, we agree with what God says about our sin and turn away from it.

As a bonus note, be aware that Satan, also known as the Accuser, often doubles back, throwing past failures in our faces. Here's a powerful Scripture for you to tuck away when you feel disqualified from God's grace. Romans 8:1 says, "There is therefore now no condemnation to those who are in Christ Jesus, who do not walk according to the flesh, but according to the Spirit."

TWO: FORGIVE OTHERS

We began by visiting God's forgiveness to us through Jesus. Now, we move into the second phrase: "And forgive us our sins, for we also forgive everyone who is indebted to us."

God views sin as debt, a gigantic loan with enormous interest we can never repay on our own. Interestingly, Jesus also describes people who sin against us as debtors, which they owe both to God and to us. It's in these moments we ask God to help us be a grace extender.

People ask me *how often* they need to forgive others. Simply put: You need to forgive as often as you want to experience the blessing of forgiveness. You and I must release others as often as necessary.

“

SIMPLY PUT: YOU NEED TO FORGIVE AS OFTEN AS YOU WANT TO EXPERIENCE THE BLESSING OF FORGIVENESS.

Peter asked Jesus this same question in Matthew 18:21: "Lord, how often shall my brother sin against me, and I forgive him? Up to seven times?" Jesus answered Peter in Matthew 18:22, "I do not say to you, up to seven times, but up to seventy times seven."

What was Jesus saying? He was telling Peter to forgive as many times as he was offended. This can be a tough pill to swallow, but this magnitude of forgiveness mirrors God's level of grace with us. Over and over again, He forgives. Followers of Christ must offer the same gift of grace to others.

Jesus uses a brilliant parable in Matthew 18:23–35 to illustrate forgiveness. In the story, a king settled up with the people who owed him money. One of his servants owed him the equivalent of ten million in today's money—basically, far more than an everyday person could pay back in their lifetime. Just as the king was going to toss the debtor and his family into prison for delinquency, the man pleaded with him, promising to repay every penny. In verse 27 we read that the king was "moved with compassion, released him, and forgave him the debt."

Amazing, right? Can you imagine the relief that man must have experienced? Certainly, he would be a grateful guy the rest of his life, treating people like the king treated him. *Unfortunately, no.* This *forgiven* man immediately finds a fellow worker who owes him about $20 in today's money, a tiny amount compared to what he owed the king, and demands to be paid. This debtor also begs for patience. However, the forgiven servant refuses and has him tossed in prison until the debt is fully repaid.

His fellow workers saw all of this play out and were outraged. They went to the king and spilled the beans—the forgiven servant had refused to forgive. It did not go well for him. The king said in verses 32 and 33, "You wicked servant! I forgave you all that debt because you begged me. Should you not also have had compassion on your fellow servant, just as I had pity on you?"

The unforgiving man was jailed and his debt reinstated. At the end of the parable in verse 35, Jesus summarizes its meaning this way: "So My heavenly Father also will do to you if each of you, from his heart, does not forgive his brother his trespasses."

The moral of the story: We are to forgive at the same level we have been forgiven. When we don't, we think we're throwing the unforgiven people in our lives into a relational debtor's prison. In reality, we're the ones in bondage. Once we realize how much we have been forgiven, we can release them. If you have trouble forgiving, through prayer ask God to give you a revelation of the price He paid for you.

Forgiveness is God's way of doing relationships. While it doesn't mean we shouldn't draw healthy boundaries with others, it does mean releasing our anger, bitterness, and resentment to God in prayer. When you do this, you will begin to sense a new power and the Presence of God in your prayer life.

THREE: MAKE THE DAILY DECISION

Forgiveness is a daily decision. It's not simply a once-in-a-while activity; it's a lifestyle. If you keep a record of wrongs and hold on to grudges, your spirit will be tormented and your prayers will be hindered.

If you are tired of experiencing painful emotions, release your offenders. Forgive those who sinned against you. Make the decision to treat others as God treats you. When you forgive, you unlock the supernatural in your life, removing the blockages to God's power. Choose to forgive every day, understanding that forgiveness is not an emotion but an act of your will.

To be honest, I had no interest in forgiving my blood father for the wounds he caused me. I clutched his sins against me in a death grip, unwilling to release him. Day after day, the Holy Spirit worked on me, nudging me, and pointing out the toll of this unforgiveness.

Finally, when I saw the depth of God's forgiveness toward me, I chose to forgive and release my father. God's love and life flowed into me like never before concerning my dad. My spiritual PVC pipe had unclogged. The most incredible part of that forgiveness journey is that I had the great privilege of leading my dad to Jesus Christ on his deathbed. Not only were we reconciled, but God used me to reconcile my father to Himself.

MAKE THE DECISION TO TREAT OTHERS AS GOD TREATS YOU.

My friends, the path to harmony in our relationships always includes forgiveness. Learn to forgive quickly to keep your heart clean and the spiritual blockages from forming. God's grace is greater than both our sin *and* desire to cling to unforgiveness. I promise, if you follow Jesus and trust God to be the ultimate Judge of rights and wrongs, you will walk as a free man or woman with fresh spiritual power in your life. And when you pray like Jesus, extending the same forgiveness to others as the Father has given you, the Holy Spirit will be active in your prayer life.

REFLECTION QUESTIONS

Before moving on to the next chapter, take some time to reflect on these questions:

- *Why do you think it is so hard to forgive some people?*
- *Consider your own life: What do you need to ask God to forgive you for today?*
- *Consider your relationships: Who do you need to forgive?*

- *How might God elevate your prayer life if you released someone in forgiveness?*
- *What did you learn from this chapter about the connection between prayer and forgiveness?*
- *Can you think of a time when you forgave someone and felt a release of God's power in your prayer life?*

CHAPTER 6:

DELIVER US

"God will always provide a way of escape."

— STEVE ROBINSON

A Vietnam War veteran once shared a story with me. He described the terror of walking through open fields between dense stretches of jungle. There were landmines hidden everywhere, but he and his fellow soldiers had to keep walking.

Though this happened decades ago halfway across the world, there are spiritual minefields we walk through every day. Thankfully, unlike those who served in Vietnam, we have a spiritual GPS inside of us pointing out these spiritual landmines.

They are areas of temptation and destructive sin waiting to explode in and around our lives. However, Jesus shows us in the next topic in the *Lord's Prayer* that we have a God who *leads* and *delivers* us from these dangers.

In Matthew 6:13, Jesus prayed, "And do not lead us into temptation, but deliver us from the evil one." We've all heard about temptation, but it's easy to overlook the second part of Christ's statement: *There is an evil one to be delivered from.* We are in a real spiritual battle against an enemy named Satan. In John 10:10a, Jesus explained his evil intentions like this: "The thief does not come except to steal, and to kill, and to destroy."

That sounds like a fight to me! However, check out what Jesus said about His own role in our lives in the very next sentence, John 10:10b: "I have come that they may have life, and that they may have it more abundantly."

Satan brings death. Jesus brings life.

No matter the landmines of temptation, the Holy Spirit will help us navigate through tumultuous pathways to a godly, abundant life. The Apostle Paul knew this as well, saying in 2 Timothy 4:18, "And the Lord will deliver me from every evil work and preserve me for His heavenly kingdom. To Him be glory forever and ever. Amen!"

To do this, God gives us access to spiritual weapons and defenses through prayer. Let's explore our spiritual arsenal to learn how the Father leads us to win this daily fight.

TWO SOURCES OF TEMPTATION

Do you know the first thing that happened when Jesus began His public ministry? The Holy Spirit led Jesus into the wilderness to fast for forty days and nights. He was physically weak, tired, and hungry. Then Matthew 4:3 happens: "Now when the tempter came to Him, he said, 'If You are the Son of God, command that these stones become bread.'"

We're going to examine this encounter. Let's start by asking, where does temptation come from? Scripture shares two sources: Satan and self.

As Jesus teaches the disciples to pray, He says, "And do not lead us into temptation." If temptation comes from Satan, why on Earth would He pray that? Does God lead us into temptation? After all, Matthew 4:2 said the Holy Spirit led Jesus into this situation where He would be tempted.

The original language gives us clarity here. A better translation of *lead us not into temptation* is, "do not allow temptation to overtake us." Jesus acknowledges temptation is all around us, but He asks that the Father not allow it to get its hooks into us.

The Apostle James also adds context to this in James 1:13, writing, "Let no one say when he is tempted, 'I am tempted by God'; for God cannot be tempted by evil, nor does He Himself tempt anyone." While God doesn't tempt us, He does allow for it to happen to test our faith. Much like lifting weights builds our physical muscles, overcoming temptation builds our spiritual muscles of faith in God—rather than in ourselves.

Did you catch that? Christianity is not an exercise in endurance against our enemy by our own power. It's about learning to press close to God in prayer, listening to the Holy Spirit's leadership to navigate the spiritual minefields we walk through.

The Apostle Paul reassures us with these words from 1 Corinthians 10:13: "No temptation has overtaken you except such as is common to man; but God is faithful, who will not allow you to be tempted beyond what you are able, but with the temptation will also make the way of escape, that you may be able to bear it."

God doesn't allow Satan to heap on more temptation than He has equipped us to escape. We see—from Genesis to Revelation—the devil is our antagonist. However, he doesn't always need as much help to tempt us as we may think. We're really good at chasing temptation on our own.

Temptation to sin also bubbles up from within. In Matthew 7:20, Jesus taught that sin isn't only outside of us in the world; it's actually inside us, as well. It's not just the evil in the world that is the problem; it's our flesh we wrestle with. And the enemy wants to take advantage of our human flesh and weakness.

If we face temptation on two fronts, inside and out, how do we win these battles?

WEAPONS AND ARMOR

You may have heard of the "whole armor of God" Paul writes about in Ephesians 6:10–20. He says it's there to help us stand against Satan's schemes because our real fight is spiritual. God equips us with spiritual weapons and armor to defeat temptation. Our job is to put the armor on every single day through prayer. There are five defensive pieces of armor and one offensive weapon available to you.

Paul was well-acquainted with the armor of a Roman soldier. When he wrote the letter to the Ephesian church, he was imprisoned in Rome. From being around many Roman soldiers, he had firsthand knowledge of what their armor looked like. Let's look at these pieces of armor one at a time and discover how to apply them in our daily prayer lives—because we certainly need them.

THE BELT OF TRUTH

In Ephesians 6:14, we read, "Stand therefore, having girded your waist with truth." Below our ribs and above our spiritual hip bones sits a belt of truth. A belt holds armor together, keeping it from sliding off; and Paul calls this belt *truth*. It is the truth of God's Word that holds everything together in our lives. Jesus called God's Word *truth* in John 17:17.

The Bible is true and vital to our daily battle with temptation. As we pray, we can ask, "God, give me faith to live by the truth of Your Word rather than the enemy's lies." After all, it was a lie that enticed Adam and Eve to sin in the garden. It was Satan questioning the *truth* of God's words. He said to Eve in Genesis 3:1, "Did God really say?"

“

GOD EQUIPS US WITH SPIRITUAL WEAPONS AND ARMOR TO DEFEAT TEMPTATION. OUR JOB IS TO PUT THE ARMOR ON EVERY SINGLE DAY THROUGH PRAYER.

The belt of truth defends our minds from the lies of the enemy and holds us together.

THE BREASTPLATE OF RIGHTEOUSNESS

In Ephesians 6:14, we learn about the next piece, the "breastplate of righteousness." The breastplate was a piece of armor worn over the chest. Organs vital to life itself were protected by the breastplate—especially our hearts. Our hearts are the deepest part of who we are.

Righteousness means a place of right standing with God, making our relationship whole. On the cross, Jesus exchanged His perfect righteousness for our sin, paying the price for eternal life (2 Corinthians 5:21). This means we can live daily, not in our own righteousness, but in the righteousness of Christ, which gives us power to overcome Satan and sin.

Satan will try to strike at our hearts and condemn us, weakening our prayer lives. But we must allow the righteousness of Christ to protect our hearts. Because, as Proverbs 4:23 says, "Keep your heart with all diligence, for out of it spring the issues of life."

This is exactly what the breastplate of righteousness does.

THE SHOES OF PEACE

The next piece of armor is found in Ephesians 6:15: "and having shod your feet with the preparation of the gospel of peace." In hand-to-hand combat, the ability to stand, sidestep, walk, run, and move freely is absolutely essential. Notice that Paul says in Ephesians 6:15 to have your feet equipped with preparation—which here means readiness.

Like a fighter in the ring with agile feet, the Holy Spirit equips us to share the gospel of peace (that ministry of reconciliation we talked about in the last chapter) with the people we meet.

Preparation makes us ready, when the opportunity comes, to invite others into a personal relationship with Jesus Christ.

The enemy wants to keep us timid, clumsy, and tripping all over ourselves with temptation. However, these gospel-ready shoes make us quick and able to do the good works God has planned for us (Ephesians 2:10).

These spiritual shoes also enable us to live in peace rather than fear. No matter the circumstances of life that threaten to knock us into anxiety, stress, and worry; we have the power to walk in peace. In Philippians 4:6–7, the Apostle Paul shares how: "Be anxious for nothing, but in everything by prayer and supplication, with thanksgiving, let your requests be made known to God; and the peace of God, which surpasses all understanding, will guard your hearts and minds through Christ Jesus."

MY FRIENDS, HOLD YOUR SHIELD HIGH AND TIGHT IN PRAYER!

As disciples, we can be ready to share the Gospel of peace because we can walk in God's supernatural peace every day.

THE SHIELD OF FAITH

When there is a fight, everyone needs a shield. In Ephesians 6:16, we are told, "Above all, taking the shield of faith with which you will be able to quench all the fiery darts of the wicked one." The shield is a piece of the armor carried on the arm or in the hand to block attacks and protect the entire body in battle. We need this because the enemy is shooting a constant barrage of fiery darts filled with accusations, temptations, and lies.

Our faith and trust in God, to fulfill His promises, are a shield that is strong enough to thwart the darts and lies of the enemy. God strengthens our faith by showing us time and again that we can stand resolute on His character and promises. Just like Proverbs 30:5 says, "Every word of God is pure; He is a shield to those who put their trust in Him."

My friends, hold your shield high and tight in prayer!

THE HELMET OF SALVATION

There are few things more dangerous than a head injury. That's why Paul tells us in Ephesians 6:17 to "take the helmet of salvation." If one of Satan's main tactics is lying, then he is certainly going to go for the headshot and try to make us doubt our salvation. Our salvation is our ultimate security, the eternal promise we will live with God forever.

Have you ever struggled with the security of your salvation? Ever worried you've not done enough to keep God's favor or love? I have wonderful news. As disciples, our confidence is not in our ability to perform perfectly—it is in the finished work of Jesus on the cross. Hebrews 10:10 gives us this assurance because Jesus's body was offered on the cross as a sacrifice "once for all." The blood of Jesus saves us. As you put on this powerful helmet, ask the Holy Spirit to move your faith from yourself to Christ where it belongs.

I love how David says it in Psalm 140:7, "O God the Lord, the strength of my salvation, You have covered my head in the day of battle." Our salvation is secure, so put on your helmet with confidence.

THE SWORD OF THE SPIRIT

Up to this point, each piece of spiritual equipment has been defensive armor. However, the last piece gives us an offensive weapon the enemy can't defend against. Ephesians 6:17 tells us we wield "the sword of the Spirit, which is the word of God." We've all seen swords—long, sharp, and sleek. They're used to stab, thrust, and swipe at an enemy. Interestingly, the sword is also a symbol of power and authority. Our sword—our power and authority—is God's Word ... spoken out of our mouths.

I said we would return to Jesus's temptation in the wilderness, and this is the perfect time. Satan came against Jesus with three temptations. Each time, do you know how Jesus responded? By declaring God's Word. His words sliced through Satan's attacks, combating the lies and offers Satan made.

I have a friend who once took his young son camping. The boy had great fun until nighttime came. The branches rustling in the wind and sticks cracking in the forest scared him. Then he remembered a Sunday school lesson about the power of Scripture. Quietly, the boy slipped his Bible out of his backpack and laid it on his chest hoping for peace to permeate his skin from the book.

While that's a good gesture, that's not how we get the Bible in our hearts! Instead, it's through declaring the truth of Scripture *from* our hearts *through* our mouths. We wield the Sword of the Spirit by speaking it in faith just like Jesus did. This is why Hebrews 4:12 says, "For the word of God is living and powerful, and sharper than any two-edged sword, piercing even to the division of soul and spirit, and of joints and marrow, and is a discerner of the thoughts and intents of the heart."

We can wield God's Word against deceit, lust, pride, and every other sinful landmine in our path. Like David said in Psalm 149:6, "Let the high praises of God be in their mouth, and a two-edged sword in their hand."

Jesus's go-to weapon of spiritual warfare was God's Word. It only makes sense we fight the same way He did. Speak the Word!

SEE THE WORD, SAY THE WORD, DO THE WORD

What is the opposite of Paul's teaching on the armor of God? If we don't wear it, we don't stand a chance. We can put it on through daily prayer in three steps:

1. We see the Word.
2. We say the Word.
3. We do the Word.

We see the Word. We set the Scriptures in front of us every day. We read the Bible, memorize it, and value it as the primary authority in our lives.

We say the Word. Like Jesus, we do more than listen; we speak it. The Scripture comes alive as it comes out of our mouth. Remember, Jesus told the devil, "It is written" before speaking the Word of truth against temptation.

We do the Word. The Bible calls us to action. James 1:22 helps us understand we're called to be "doers of the word, and not hearers only, deceiving yourselves." Disciples take action on what God teaches through His Word.

As you apply the whole armor of God daily, the Holy Spirit will help you navigate the countless spiritual landmines of temptation. You can walk the fields of life with confidence and security. My friends, this is the path to victory over any temptation.

REFLECTION QUESTIONS

Before moving on to the next chapter, take some time to reflect on these questions:

- *What did you learn about temptation in this chapter?*
- *How are you planning to apply the whole armor of God in your life?*

- *Which pieces of spiritual armor will be most powerful to you? Why?*
- *What areas of temptation in your life do you need victory in today?*
- *What did you learn from this chapter about the connection between spiritual armor and victory in temptation?*

CHAPTER 7:

YOURS IS THE GLORY

"As we trust in God's Word, exalt Jesus with our lips, and give the Holy Spirit a place to work in us— we can expect supernatural grace and glory to flow through our lives."

— STEVE ROBINSON

I once heard a story about a pastor who noticed a sign in a pet shop window: *Christian Horse for Sale.* Since the pastor owned a ranch, he was immediately interested and went into the shop. The owner took him out back where he met a beautiful Arabian stallion.

The owner agreed to let the pastor take a test ride; so he hopped in the saddle, grabbed the reins, and yelled, "Giddyap!"

The horse ignored him.

"No, no," counseled the horse's owner, "this is a Christian horse. If you want him to move, you must say, 'Praise the Lord!'"

The pastor did as he was told and the horse started off on a leisurely walk. However, he soon found that the horse refused to stop.

The pastor looked at the owner, confused.

The owner cupped his hands around his mouth and called out, "You need to say, 'Amen!'"

"Amen," the pastor said firmly. The horse stopped.

The pastor decided that he liked the horse, so he bought him and took him home to his ranch in the country. The next day, he saddled the horse up and said, "Praise the Lord." The horse started to trot and they rode into the countryside. Suddenly, the horse saw a rattlesnake crossing the path. Frightened, he reared and bolted straight for a cliff.

The pastor cried, "Whoa!" but the horse only ran faster. In vain, he tried one word after another. He just couldn't remember the command to stop the horse.

Finally, he remembered and screamed, "AMEN!" just as the horse approached the edge of the cliff. The horse skidded to a stop, halting just before the pair hurtled over the edge.

The pastor was so grateful to be alive that he leaned back in the saddle, raised his hands to the sky, and shouted, "Praise the Lord!"

They tumbled head over hooves, landing in a heap. The pastor moaned, "Amen."

In this chapter we explore the final topic in the *Lord's Prayer*: praise. However, I promise it won't be as hazardous to our health as it was to our fictitious pastor. In Matthew 6:13, Jesus concluded, praying, "For Yours is the kingdom and the power and the glory forever. Amen."

Jesus opened and closed His teaching on prayer with praise. Simple prayer is God-centered, starting and ending with God. Jesus showed us that prayer is about God the Father first and forever because all of our life should be filled with praise, worship, and honor for God's glory.

Praise is declaring Who God is to you and over your life. Jesus gave us three areas to praise the Father for: His Kingdom reign, His unlimited power, and His eternal glory.

"

SIMPLE PRAYER IS GOD-CENTERED, STARTING AND ENDING WITH GOD.

YOURS IS THE KINGDOM

In Chapter Three, we learned that the Kingdom of God is *the rule and reign of God in the hearts of His people.* It is the sphere of His rule, unconfined by a physical space or geographical region. God's Kingdom is a form of spiritual government where we are His people, submitted to His authority. However, there is mystery in this Kingdom.

It is *invisible, yet tangible.* Jesus encourages us to receive and participate in His invisible Kingdom. In fact, in Luke 12:32, He said, "Do not fear, little flock, for it is your Father's good pleasure to give you the kingdom." The Kingdom of God is full of peace, joy, and righteousness—it is also an unshakeable foundation to build your life upon. This means everything we have, everything we are, and everything we do is to honor God.

WHAT WE BELIEVE IN OUR HEARTS AND CONFESS WITH OUR MOUTHS, WE ACT ON WITH OUR HANDS.

The Kingdom consists of inside-out living. What we believe in our hearts and confess with our mouths, we act on with our hands. Our faith is dynamic, leading to good works as Kingdom people (James 2:26). Obedient living brings glory to God. Jesus praises His Father in prayer, teaching His disciples to acknowledge and fully submit to God's Kingdom authority.

This is also about praise. Jesus shows the disciples how to *declare* God's glory. He is the Creator of the heavens and earth. He is in control of our lives and we are in the palm of His hands. He owns it all, rules it all, and sustains it all.

Jesus began with praise and ended with declaration, adoration, and worship.

YOURS IS THE POWER

Next, Jesus declared that God rules with unparalleled power. When we pray, we are speaking with the One Who spoke the universe into existence from nothing (Genesis 1:1). Everything we see is a direct result of His power to create. If you ever need a reminder of God's power, take a drive into the countryside on a clear evening, away from all of the lights, noise, and distraction, and look up.

I remember taking each of my kids to a father-child event in northern California. We camped out in the wilderness, gathering around the fire, telling stories, and talking about life. Each time, one of my favorite moments was looking up at the innumerable stars sprinkled across the night sky. Each time I thought, *Wow, God is big!* And even more amazing, He knows them all by name (Psalm 147:4).

In Psalm 19:1–4, David wrote:

> *The heavens declare the glory of God;*
> *And the firmament shows His handiwork.*
> *Day unto day utters speech,*
> *And night unto night reveals knowledge.*
> *There is no speech nor language*
> *Where their voice is not heard.*
> *Their line has gone out through all the earth,*
> *And their words to the end of the world.*

Isn't that beautiful? David says creation is the universal language praising God, revealing knowledge about His power, and declaring His glory! Jesus invites us to join the heavens in praising the Father, who is the Source of all power.

How often, even as children of the all-powerful God, do we also find ourselves at the end of our strength? The God we praise is the same Good Father who makes His limitless resources available to us.

As we discovered in the last chapter, the Apostle Paul instructs us to be conduits of God's power in Ephesians 6:10: "Be strong in the Lord and in the power of His might." As you pray, thank God your Father for inviting you to be a participant in His power. As we praise Him, He pours His power and strength into our lives.

Although our own power is limited, God's is not. There is never a valley God cannot lift us out of. His power is limitless and never runs dry. I agree with Jesus: a God like that is worth glorifying!

YOURS IS THE GLORY

What does it mean to glorify God? To start, glory is defined as renown, honor, or magnificence; and we find it most fully in the Person of God Himself. The Old Testament word for glory is *kabod*, and it means "honor and weightiness." It is also used to congratulate someone for a job well done. Jesus is encouraging us in the final words of this prayer to declare God's glory over our lives and glorify Him by how we live. He invited His disciples (and us today) to be vessels of His glory. Not only is His glory *out there* in creation, but it also comes to live inside us.

In 2 Chronicles 5:13–14, we read about God's glory filling up physical space. The people were worshiping through music in total unity, singing, "*For He is* good, for His mercy *endures* forever." Then, "the house of the Lord was filled with a cloud, so that the priests could not continue ministering because of the cloud; for the glory of the Lord filled the house of God."

God's presence showed up so tangibly there wasn't even room for people to stand. When the presence of God is manifested in an environment, you can feel it. In other words, we can sense the glory of God—because it is *real.* Praise and worship invite God's presence and glory into *any* location.

“

WHEN WE PRAISE HIM, GOD’S PRESENCE MEETS US WHERE WE ARE.

When we praise Him, God's presence meets us where we are. This is because He loves us as His children and desires closeness with you and me. We can expect God's glory to rest upon our lives every day. In your prayer time, open your mouth wide. Sing to Him, glorify Him, and don't worry about it; no one's around to hear you! Let Him fill you with His glory!

PRAISE HIM EVERY DAY

Though Jesus shows us prayer begins and ends by praising God, it's important to remember that God doesn't simply want praise from us, He wants a relationship with us. Like a good Father, God wants to talk with His kids. *Prayer is a dialogue, not a monologue.*

PRAYER IS A CONSTANT CONVERSATION ABOUT THE DEEPEST FACETS OF LIFE.

The *Lord's Prayer* is a wonderful pattern for that conversation. Patterns help us in life. Just like weekly dates with our spouse, special trips with our kids, or frequent dinners with dear friends, regular time with God is the perfect pattern for a life filled with spiritual power.

Prayer is more than a one-and-done session when times are difficult or at the end of a church service. Prayer is a constant conversation about the deepest facets of life. My heart for you is to meet God in these amazing places and to experience the renewal He has for you.

I have prayed this pattern almost every morning for over thirty years, and it has kept my heart, mind, and actions centered on God. Connecting with God as my power Source has fueled my faith, life, and spiritual growth.

Here is my daily invitation to you:

1. Believe you can have a powerful prayer life.
2. Meet God as your Good Father.

3. Invite God's Kingdom power into your daily life.
4. Trust God for your daily bread, believing He'll provide everything you need.
5. Unblock your spiritual PVC pipe by extending the same forgiveness to others God has extended to you.
6. Ask God to help you navigate the spiritual landmines of temptation.
7. Start and end your prayer time with praise.

As you meet God like this, the Holy Spirit will draw you deeper into relationship with Him. There will be seasons where interceding for your church and community is heavy on your heart. Other times you will desperately need God's provision in your life. Praying through this pattern will touch every area of your life and serve your ongoing conversation with our Father.

What's next? Pray every day and teach someone else to pray like Jesus, as well. Share this book with others. Use the prayer pattern resource at the end of this book to help yourself and others. After all, how did my son learn to tie his shoes? My wife and I had to teach him. The basis of this entire book has been Jesus's heart to model and mentor the kind of prayer life that'll change not just you, but the lives of those around you.

REFLECTION QUESTIONS

As you finish your study of the *Lord's Prayer*, take some time to reflect on these questions:

- *What did you learn about praising God?*
- *How were you encouraged to worship, praise, and give God glory?*
- *What are three ways you can more consistently praise God each day?*
- *What can you praise God for right now?*

- *What would experiencing God's presence in your life mean to you?*
- *What did you learn from this chapter about the connection between praising God and letting His glory fill your life?*

YOUR SIMPLE PATTERN TO PRAY LIKE JESUS EVERY DAY

This outline is your daily guide to pray the *Lord's Prayer.* You can earmark it or even rip it out and slip it into your Bible. Blessings as you incorporate Jesus's prayer pattern into your daily life!

1. *OUR FATHER IN HEAVEN, HALLOWED BE YOUR NAME.*

Meet God as your Good Father through Jesus, looking up, not in. Pray His names and declare His promises in your life.

Jehovah-Tsidkenu: *The LORD, my righteousness.*	**Jehovah-Rapha:** *The Lord, my healer.*
Jehovah-Mekaddishkem: *The Lord, my sanctification.*	**Jehovah-Jireh:** *The Lord, my provision.*
Jehovah-Shammah: *The Lord is near.*	**Jehovah-Nissi:** *The Lord, my banner.*
Jehovah-Shalom: *The Lord, my peace.*	**Jehovah-Roi:** *The Lord, my shepherd.*

2. YOUR KINGDOM COME. YOUR WILL BE DONE ON EARTH AS IT IS IN HEAVEN.

Pray for God's rule, reign, and will to come to pass in yourself, your family, your church, and your nation.

3. GIVE US DAY BY DAY OUR DAILY BREAD.

Pray specifically for your personal needs as well as other people's.

4. AND FORGIVE US OUR DEBTS, AS WE FORGIVE OUR DEBTORS.

Ask God to forgive you, and then extend that forgiveness to others. Make the decision to eliminate the toxin of unforgiveness in your life.

5. AND DO NOT LEAD US INTO TEMPTATION, BUT DELIVER US FROM THE EVIL ONE.

Put on your spiritual armor (Ephesians 6:10–18):

The Belt of Truth	The Helmet of Salvation
The Breastplate of Righteousness	The Sword of the Spirit
The Shield of Faith	Shoes Ready to Share the Gospel

6. FOR YOURS IS THE KINGDOM AND THE POWER AND THE GLORY FOREVER. AMEN.

Give God praise, honor, and glory as your Creator, Redeemer, and King!

ABOUT THE AUTHOR

Stephen J. Robinson is a pastor, speaker, and author. As founder and senior pastor, he has led Church of the King into an impactful ministry of thousands across six physical locations, Real Life radio program, online streaming, and television.

He is a graduate of Tulane University, holds a master's degree from King's Seminary, and is a doctoral student at Southeastern University in Lakeland, Florida. He is the author of *Simple Prayer, Not OK?, If Only ... , Above The Noise, The Other Side, Born For This*, and *Restart*.

Pastor Steve and his wife, Jennifer, live in Mandeville, Louisiana and are blessed with four children—Isabelle, Conrad, William, and Annaliese.

ChurchoftheKing.com

Made in the USA
Columbia, SC
01 November 2021

47989368R00048